Thebes: The History and Legacy of the Ancient Greek City-State

By Charles River Editors

A piece of 7th century BCE art from Thebes

About Charles River Editors

Charles River Editors is a boutique digital publishing company, specializing in bringing history back to life with educational and engaging books on a wide range of topics. Keep up to date with our new and free offerings with this 5 second sign up on our weekly mailing list, and visit Our Kindle Author Page to see other recently published Kindle titles.

We make these books for you and always want to know our readers' opinions, so we encourage you to leave reviews and look forward to publishing new and exciting titles each week.

Introduction

A picture of the ruins of Thebes' central fortress

Thebes

Dominated to this day by the sprawling white marble complex of the Acropolis, Athens is a city which is immensely and rightly proud of its past. For a period of roughly three centuries, the polis of Athens stood, if not in a position of unchallenged supremacy among the cities of Hellas, then at the very least among its three most important polities. Its fledgling Empire, though small by the standards later set by Alexander or the Romans, or even by those of its ancient enemy Persia, nonetheless encompassed cities as far afield as Asia Minor and Southern Italy, a remarkable fact considering such expansion was achieved by the inhabitants of a single city and its immediate surroundings, rather than by an entire nation. In virtually all fields of human endeavor Athens was so much at the forefront of dynamism and innovation that the products of its most brilliant minds remain not only influential but entirely relevant to this day. In the field of medicine, the great physician Hippocrates not only advanced the practical knowledge of human anatomy and care-giving but changed the entire face of the medical profession. The great philosophers of Athens, men like Aristotle, Socrates, and Plato, interrogated themselves with startling complexity about the nature of good and evil, questioned the existence of divinity, advocated intelligent design, and went so far as to argue that all life was composed of infinitesimal particles. Great architects and sculptors such as Phidias produced works of art of such breathtaking realism and startling dynamism that they later formed the driving force behind the resurgence of sculpture during the Renaissance and served as masters to artists such as Michelangelo, Bernini, and Donatello. The plays of dramatists such as Aristophanes not only displayed an acerbic wit and a genius for political satire so pronounced that their works continue to be performed – and topical – to this day, but served as the inspiration for virtually all playwrights from Shakespeare to the present day. And this does not take into account the host of equally brilliant mathematicians, natural philosophers, historians, astronomers and politicians that the city's great schools nurtured and produced.

The most unique city-state in Ancient Greece was probably Sparta, which continues to fascinate contemporaneous society. It is not entirely clear why Sparta placed such a great emphasis on having a militaristic society, but the result was that military fitness was a preoccupation from birth. If a Spartan baby did not appear physically fit at birth, it was left to die. Spartan children underwent military training around the age of 7 years old, and every male had to join the army around the age of 18. The Spartans, whose carefully constructed approach to warfare and – there is no other word for it – Spartan way of life, earned the grudging admiration of all of Greece and succeeded in establishing themselves in the years following the reforms of the semi-legendary ruler Lycurgus as the greatest military force in all of Hellas.

Modern perceptions of Classical Greece are almost invariably based on Athens and Sparta, but Thebes was also a key player in the history of the region in this pivotal period. Indeed, it was, in fact, Thebes that was the major power for many of the years preceding the emergence of Macedon.

The reasons for so little being known about Thebes and its contributions to ancient Greek civilization are complex, but the fact that it was totally destroyed by Alexander the Great is certainly one. Unlike Athens and Sparta, there are no magnificent structures still extant; indeed, the scale of the destruction meted out to Thebes was so great that very few artifacts of any kind have been discovered that enable a full picture of life in the city. With the very notable exception of Pindar, Thebes did not produce significant numbers of philosophers or playwrights, nor did it host any major pan-Hellenic festivals. Consequently, Thebes is not as well-known as the other major players in the Greek world at that time. It is also true that Thebes was not the most loved of the Greek poleis, and its reputation never really recovered from its decision to side with the Persians during the Persians' invasion of the Greek mainland.

Those points notwithstanding, Thebes was an important city-state, served as the scene of many of the great myths of Greece, and developed a reputation for military might and tactical genius that was well-deserved. Thebes' association, at least in the eyes of contemporary Classical Greek rivals, with male homosexuality is a topic in its own right, and a study of the Sacred Band that proved so vital in Thebes' victories in the Classical period is especially revealing, though there is no proof of any real substance that Theban attitudes were greatly different than those of other

Greeks on the whole issue of what was and was not acceptable. Regardless, Thebes' rise and fall are subjects well worthy of study, and ones that provide invaluable insights into how ancient Greek politics worked, especially in relation to the constantly changing pattern of alliances. Thebes also provided inspirational stories of individual and group heroism in the face of huge odds.

Thebes: The History and Legacy of the Ancient Greek City-State examines the history of one of Greece's most important poleis. Along with pictures depicting important people, places, and events, you will learn about Thebes like never before.

Thebes: The History and Legacy of the Ancient Greek City-State
About Charles River Editors
Introduction
   The Origins of Thebes
   The 5th Century
   Epaminondas and Pelopidas
   The Sacred Band
   The Aftermath of Leuctra
   The Decline of Thebes
   Online Resources
   Further Reading
Free Books by Charles River Editors
Discounted Books by Charles River Editors

The Origins of Thebes

Thebes was situated in Boeotia, 30 miles to the northwest of Athens, in a plain between Lake Hylica and the Cithaeron Mountains, which divided Boeotia from Attica. The plain was approximately 700 feet above sea level, and as was normal with Greek cities, Thebes was built around an *acropolis*. The Theban Acropolis was situated on a low ridge dividing the surrounding fertile plain that was well served by abundant springs, the most famous of these being named 'Dirce'.

Tradition has it that Thebes was originally founded by the Ectenians under the leadership of Ogyges, or Ogygus. Some of the earliest references to the city name it "Ogygion". Pausanias, in his *Description of Greece*, wrote, "The first to occupy the land of Thebes are said to have been the Ectenians whose king was Ogygus, an aboriginal. From his name is derived Ogygian which is an epithet of Thebes used by most of the poets. The Ectenes, they say perished by pestilence and after them there settled in the land Hyantes and the Aones who I think were Boeotian tribes and not foreigners."[1]

Generally, however, in mythology, the city was founded by Cadmus, the brother of Europa, Cilix, and Phoenix, son of Agenor and Telephassa of Tyre and an ancestor of Oedipus. This genealogy explains why the citadel, founded at the beginning of the city, was known as the Cadmea. Legend placed Cadmus as the first Greek hero and, alongside Perseus and Bellerophon, the greatest of the monster slayers before Hercules.[2] He was believed to have been a Phoenician prince whose sister, Europa, was abducted. He was sent by his parents to rescue her, and on his travels—depending on which version of the tale is read—he either founded the city on instructions from Delphi or on the instructions of Athena.

In the latter version, Cadmus defeated a giant serpent or dragon guarding the spring of Areia. Athena told Cadmus to sow the serpent's teeth into the ground, and from these sprang the warriors, the Spartoi, meaning the "sown". For reasons that are not entirely clear in the mythology, Cadmus threw a stone amongst them, they fought each other until only five survived, and it was these *spartoi* who founded Thebes with Cadmus and built the Cadmea.

---

[1] Pausanias, *Description of Greece*, 9.5.1.
[2] P. 75, *The Heroes of the Greeks* by K. Kerenyi (1959). London.

A Peter Paul Rubens workshop painting of Cadmus sowing the dragon teeth

An ancient depiction of Cadmus fighting the dragon

In the former version, Delphi had ordered him to follow a sacred cow until it fell exhausted and build a city where it lay, and the encounter with the dragon only occurred after that event. In both versions, however, Ares, to whom the dragon was sacred, was incensed by Cadmus's actions and insisted on Cadmus undergoing eight years of penance serving him. When his period of penance was over, he married Harmonia, with whom he had a son, Polydorus, and four daughters: Agave, Autonoe, Ino, and Semele.

The wedding of Cadmus and Harmonia was a grand event attended by all the gods. Despite all this divine attention, Cadmus's reign did not go well, and he eventually abdicated in favor of his grandson, Pentheus, and went off to Illyria, becoming king there and founding the city of Lychnidos. The curse that had followed Cadmus for slaying the sacred dragon followed him throughout his life, and in desperation, he asked the gods to turn him into a serpent; the gods granted his wish and that of Harmonia, who wished to share her husband's fate. The whole tale of Cadmus and Harmonia is shrouded in symbolism, one of the most potent being the idea of the marriage of Cadmus and Harmonia symbolizing the joining of Phoenician learning with the Greek love of beauty.

Cadmus was credited by Herodotus with introducing the Greek alphabet from Phoenicia.[3] He also dated Cadmus quite precisely to around 2000 B.C.[4] based on his own calculations of Cadmean inscriptions in the Temple of Apollo at Thebes. The inscriptions were on tripods from the time of Laius, the great-grandson of Cadmus, and it was from this information that he made his guess as to when Cadmus had lived and founded Thebes.[5]

Herodotus's dating of the founding of Thebes reflected the general consensus among Greeks on this point, placing the beginnings of the city, therefore, to well before the Trojan War, in the Aegean Bronze Age. This dating, however, does not sit well with modern understandings of the spread of the Phoenician and Greek alphabets, which date to the late 9th century B.C. The Phoenician alphabet was not fully developed until approximately 1050 B.C., after the collapse of the Bronze Age. The connection of Cadmus, in this context as a substitute for general Phoenician influence, to either the development of either Linear B or the later Phoenician alphabet is tenuous, but it is interesting to note that in modern-day Lebanon, Cadmus is still accepted as the "carrier of the letter" to the world. Today, despite the obviously mythical tales surrounding Cadmus, there is an emerging view in the academic world that he was an actual historical figure and that the oral tales contain a solid core of genealogical and narrative truth.[6]

Cadmus's daughter, Semele, is the heroine of yet another popular myth from the Classical age. Semele was seduced by Zeus in the Cadmea, and Hera, not noted for tolerance in relation to her husband's mortal lovers, tricked Semele into asking to see Zeus in his full glory, whereupon she was consumed by his brilliance. Zeus, however, managed to save the child Semele was carrying by him, and in due course, Dionysius was born. Later, Dionysius brought his mother from the underworld to Mount Olympus, where she was accepted by the gods, though no doubt with some reluctance on Hera's part. Dionysius visited Thebes to honor his mother, only to be thrown in prison by the king at the time, Pentheus, who did not know Dionysius was a new god. Dionysius took his revenge by making some Theban women mad, and they tore the unfortunate king to pieces. Pausanias, when he visited Thebes, was shown the bedchamber where Dionysius was reputedly conceived.[7]

---

[3] Herodotus, *Histories*, Book V 58.
[4] Herodotus, *Histories*, Book II 2.145.
[5] Herodotus, *Histories*, Book V 59.1.
[6] p.15, *A Concise History of Ancient Greece* by P. Green (1974). London.
[7] *Dionysos: Archetypal Image of the Indestructible Life* by C. Kerenyi (1976). Princeton.

A Theban coin depicting Dionysius

Another important figure in Greek mythology associated with Thebes was King Laius, already referred to above. He was a divine hero, the son of Labdacus, but raised by Lycus after the death of his father. Legend had it that Amphion and Zethus took the throne from Laius, the legitimate descendant and heir of Cadmus, while he was still an infant. Supporters of the Cadmean line secreted him out of the city, and Laius found refuge with King Pelops of Pisa.[8] He did not exactly repay this generosity in later life, raping Chrysippus, Pelops's son, and carrying him off to Thebes. This abduction is generally believed to have been the subject of a tragedy by Euripides that has since been lost. Laius's rape of Chrysippus was believed by many 5th-century B.C. commentators to be the first instance of homosexuality among mortals and may have provided the rationale for pedagogic pederasty, a practice for which Thebes was known at the time.

After the rape of Chrysippus, Laius married Jocasta, but the oracle at Delphi warned him that he must not have a child with her, as any offspring would kill him and marry his wife. Despite the warning, after a night drinking heavily, Laius fathered Oedipus. He ordered the child to be exposed on Mount Cithaeron, but the child was saved by a shepherd who gave him to King Polybus and Queen Merope of Corinth, who raised him.[9] As a young adult, Oedipus consulted the oracle at Delphi about his parents and was warned not to return home, as he would kill his father and marry his mother. Oedipus assumed that the warnings referred to Polybus, and so he set out for Thebes rather than return to Corinth. By chance, he met Laius on the road. Laius was

---

[8] Pausanias, *Description of Greece*, 9.5.6; Apollodotous Library, 3.5.5.
[9] Apollodorus Library, 3.5.7.

himself traveling to Delphi to consult the Pythia. At a point in the road known as Cleft Way, the two met, and Oedipus refused to give way to the king, whereupon Laius drove his chariot wheel over the foot of someone he considered an upstart. Oedipus killed him and his attendants.

Carrying on to Thebes, he found the city being terrorized by the Sphinx. The Sphinx had the head of a woman and the winged body of a lion. She reportedly vowed that she would terrorize the city until her riddle was solved. The riddle posed the question as to what creature might have two, three, or four feet, could move in air, water, and land, and moved more slowly the more feet it had. Oedipus solved the riddle by identifying man as the creature being described, whereupon the Sphinx, in a rage, threw herself to her death from the Acropolis in Thebes. Oedipus assumed the vacant throne and in due course married the missing king's wife, still unaware that he had married his mother. It was only many years later that he learned the truth. As with so many of the descendants of Cadmus, Oedipus met with a tragic end, and Thebes seemed destined to be continually cursed by the transgressions of her royal line.

In mythology, Thebes was also the birthplace of Hercules. He was the son of Zeus, who had disguised himself as the Theban general Amphytrion to seduce his wife, Alcmene, a descendant of Perseus. Hera tormented Hercules throughout his life, furiously jealous of Alcmene, as she was of all Zeus's mortal lovers. Amphytrion returned to Thebes the same night as Zeus had impregnated his wife, and she conceived another child by him at that time, Iphicles. Iphicles was the father of Hercules's charioteer, Iolaus, in a rare case of what is termed heteropaternal superfecundation.

Classical Numismatic Group, Inc.'s picture of a Theban coin depicting Hercules

There are numerous other mythological tales based on Thebes, one of the best known being that recounted by Aeschylus in the *Seven Against Thebes*. The legend stated that a war broke out between the two sons of Oedipus, Polyneikes and Eteokles. The former had been banished by the latter, after which Polyneikes allied with the Achaeans to take the city. When scaling the walls, six of the seven champions, including Polyneikes, were killed, but the attack was successful, and the Cadmeans of Thebes were forced to flee to the north. The myth is regarded today as a symbolic metaphor for the general regression of Greek civilization following the end of the Mycenaean period.

Myths relating to the Theban royal family rarely ended well, and the tale of another Theban queen, Niobe, recounted by Boccaccio, is no exception.[10] The queen was apparently so taken with her own success at producing 14 children that she demanded the citizens sacrifice to her rather than the Olympians. The gods took their revenge by killing all her offspring, and she, in her grief, turned into a stone pillar. This type of cautionary tale of the perils of hubris and defiance of the gods is not uncommon in Greek mythology, but it is certainly noticeable how many are centered on Thebes.

Separating fact from fiction is not always straightforward in the case of Thebes, but it is now generally felt that the area of Boeotia upon which Thebes was built was inhabited at least from 3000 B.C. The modern town lies directly on top of any remains that might be left after the sacking of the city by Alexander, so firm archaeological evidence is extremely limited. There is evidence, however, of third millennium fortifications, paved courtyards, some mud brick walls, and basic drains. From 2500 B.C., evidence has been found of wool and food production along with grinding stones, loom weights, and bronze carpentry tools.

There is also convincing evidence of fairly widespread trade from this period, based on the discovery of gold, silver, ivory, and Cycladic vessels. From 2000 B.C., there is evidence of expansion, with stone cists and pits and shaft graves being used, some of which contained precious goods.

The building of the seven-gated Theban wall is attributed in mythology to Amphion, who it is said charmed the stones into place by playing his lyre to them.[11] The more factual evidence suggests that walls were constantly upgraded from 1700 B.C. onwards, and that Thebes reached its Bronze Age peak at around 1400 B.C. It is from this period that the ruined Minoan-style palace at Cadmea dates; the building was adorned with paintings of Theban women in Minoan dress, and further archaeological evidence in the form of Cretan vases in the area confirm well-developed contacts between the Minoans and Thebans. In 1964, a Mesopotamian cylinder was discovered dating from the 1400s B.C., which strengthened the evidence for the theory that writing spread from the East to Greece through Thebes in this period. In 1970, clay tablets confirmed that there were strong links between the Mycenaean and Minoan civilizations and that Thebes played a prominent role in these links. These close links with the Middle East and the islands of the Mediterranean suggested a polis that was far from the insular city-states that were

---

[10] Boccaccio, *Famous Women* (Trans. V. Brown (2003). Harvard
[11] Pausanias, *Description of Greece*, 6.20.18.

so common throughout Greece at this time.

In terms of what the city may have looked like in this period, evidence is very sparse. Homer described some of the fortifications in *The Iliad*, and there is archaeological evidence of stone-built aqueducts and terracotta pipes dating from this period. From the 13th century B.C., chamber tombs with benches and drains have been discovered, a few with wall paintings and grave goods. There is very strong evidence that at some point in the city's history, it was badly damaged by fire and a series of earthquakes. There is very little information at all about the city during the Greek Dark Ages (1000-700 B.C.), and it is only in the 7th century B.C. that Thebes re-emerged as a major player on the Greek mainland and became a constant rival to both Athens and Sparta for hegemony in Hellas.

The 5th Century

Homer refers to Seven Gated Thebes in *The Iliad*,[12] and the city came into prominence in terms of Greek politics by the late 6th century B.C. At this time, Thebes came into direct conflict with Athens over the state of Plataea. Thebes wished to incorporate the polis into its own lands, but the Plataeans called for help from Athens in maintaining their independence.

The Theban attempt to take Plataea was unsuccessful, but it left the Thebans with a simmering resentment against Athens that may partly explain why the Thebans later supported the Persian emperor Xerxes in his invasion of Attica.[13] Despite the victory in the First Persian War, it was felt that, maybe not in the next year or even in the next decade, the Persians would come again. The Spartan king Leonidas was the main advocate of this theory, sustaining it even when Darius died and was succeeded by his son Xerxes in 486 B.C. Under Leonidas and their other king, Agesilaus, the Spartans waged a series of campaigns in the years following the Battle of Marathon to bring reluctant allies and Persian sympathizers into the fold and ensure a united Greek front would greet all Persian attempts to invade.

That invasion, just as Leonidas had prophesied, came in 480 B.C., when Xerxes, at the head of an army which Herodotus claimed numbered over a million men, bridged the Hellespont (the Dardanelles straits) via a colossal pontoon bridge and marched his army into Thrace, threatening Greece proper. All eyes turned to the Spartans, but the Spartans dithered. It is unclear what prompted the Spartan reluctance to take the field. Some historians have suggested that, being chiefly concerned with the Peloponnese, the Spartans wanted to defend the Isthmus of Corinth, and let the rest of Greece fend for itself. Others accept the official Spartan reason that as a deeply religious people they could not ignore the Olympic proscription, in vigor at that particular time of year, that forbade Greek cities from marching in arms.

Whatever the reason, the Spartans could field only a token force: accordingly, they sent an "all-

---

[12] Homer, *Iliad*, Book IV 406.
[13] Herodotus, *Histories*, VII 204.

sire" suicide unit of three hundred full Spartiates, notionally the King's bodyguard, under Leonidas, to defend the pass at Thermopylae in north-eastern Greece. These 300 were bolstered by 600 *perioikoi* or "neighbors" (literally "those nearby"), line infantry of lesser prestige from the towns surrounding Sparta, and a further 900 helot light infantrymen, one for each hoplite. They were also joined by between 3,000-5,000 thousand allied Greeks from Corinth, Arcadia, Mantinea, Tegea, Thespiae, Phokis, Locris, and others.

For three days, Leonidas, his Three Hundred, and their allies withstood wave upon wave of Persian attacks, inflicting more than 20,000 casualties upon the enemy. Finally, outflanked and exhausted, they were defeated; Leonidas sent all the allies in retreat save for the remnant of the Three Hundred, but the Thespian soldiers refused to leave, taking up their places beside the Three Hundred. According to Herodotus, during their legendary last stand, after their weapons and armor were smashed and broken the Greeks fought on with nails and teeth before being at last cut down to the last man.

Thebes sent a contingent of 400 to fight alongside the Spartans at Thermopylae, and they, like the more famous Spartan 300, were all killed. It was after that battle that the Thebans changed to support Xerxes and fought with the Persians at the Battle of Plataea in 479 B.C.[14] The Greeks were furious at what they regarded as Theban treachery, and the city was subsequently deprived of its presidency of the Boeotian League.

Given the magnitude of its involvement with Persia, it might be assumed that Thebes would have suffered much more severely than it did, but Greek politics intervened to save Thebes from further humiliation. The period between 479 B.C. and 431 B.C. (known as the *Pentacoetia*) and to some extent the decades that followed, although they were marred by the harrow of the Peloponnesian War, were the golden age of Athens. The victory over the Persians ushered in an era of burgeoning confidence and dynamism that made the Athenians feel invincible, as well as ushering in a fresh wave of democratization. Salamis, Athens's most dazzling triumph, had not been the product of the gentlemen-rankers of the heavy infantry but of the lowest of the working classes, the oarsmen and marines of the Athenian fleet, and they reveled in their status as preservers of Hellenic freedom and spoke forth with unprecedented vigor in the *Ecclesia*. The Acropolis, which had been destroyed by Xerxes, was rebuilt into the dazzling spectacle that still stands to this day, while under the auspices of the great sculptor Phidias the mighty buildings were decorated with sculpture of unprecedented grace and beauty. At the same time, colossal walls miles long were built to link Athens to the port of the Piraeus, meaning that Athens could never be besieged by land forces alone.

The inevitable war broke out in 460 B.C., splitting Greece down the middle and forcing most of the great *poleis* to align themselves with Sparta or Athens. At the time, however, Sparta itself was unable to field a significant force due to being occupied at home with mopping up the helot

---

[14] Herodotus, *Histories*, VII 32.

revolt. That also required leaving much of the Spartan army on standby in case of further uprisings.

The main Spartan achievement in what became later known as the First Peloponnesian War (the prelude to the far more devastating Second Peloponnesian War) was a victory over Athens at Tanagra in 457 B.C. At that battle, the Spartan army had supported the Boeotians in preserving their independence, but after the victory they decamped, allowing Athens to take over the region anyway. This caused a scandal in Sparta, ending with the exile of the two kings for supineness, and Sparta was forced to call for a somewhat embarrassing five-year treaty with Athens to recover its strength in the wake of the revolt. It has been suggested that it was around this time that some elements of the *perioikoi* were incorporated into the Spartan line infantry to make up for manpower shortage, although this is an issue of some contention. More importantly, Sparta signed a 30 year peace with its old rival Argos, ensuring it was free to pursue hostilities with Athens when the time came.

As a result, attempts by Sparta to have Thebes thrown out of the Delphic *amphictyony* were blocked by Athens, which was more concerned with curbing Spartan influence than punishing Thebes. In due course, in 457 B.C., Sparta supported Thebes' reinstatement as the major power in Boeotia, as it needed a counterbalance to Athenian influence in central Greece. Thebes became involved in the Peloponnesian War and was a firm ally of Sparta in the conflict. Sparta helped Thebes in the destruction of Plataea in 427 B.C., and, in 424 B.C., they inflicted a severe defeat on Athens at the Battle of Delium.

It was at the Battle of Delium that the unique Theban military organization and tactics that later gave them hegemony in Hellas first came to the fore. Despite having supported Sparta throughout the war, enduring Athenian ravaging of Boeotia and a siege of the Cadmea, Sparta was not minded to treat Thebes particularly well at the end of the war. Thebes was incensed when Sparta refused Theban demands to annex certain poleis and made it clear that it would protect those cities against any Theban aggression. In 404 B.C., the Thebans had urged the Spartans to raze Athens to the ground, but within a year, Thebes was secretly working for the restoration of the democracy in Athens, Theban policy now being to negate any attempt by its erstwhile ally to dominate Greece.

Epaminondas and Pelopidas

In the wake of the Peloponnesian War, the Spartans began to harbor imperialistic ambitions again. They openly supported Cyrus, who had enjoyed a friendly relationship with Lysander, in his attempt to seize the throne of Persia from his older brother Artaxerxes, and even though he was killed at Cunaxa the Spartans used an appeal for help from the Ionians (so often previously rebuffed) and invaded Anatolia. However, their army was crushed by Artaxerxes at Cnidus in 394 B.C., apparently causing a sigh of relief from the Ionian cities who felt Spartan rule would be even more oppressive than subjugation to Persia.

Despite its apparent position of supremacy, Sparta was actually rotting from within. The Spartiate warriors who constituted the backbone of the political establishment and the flower of the army had shrunk in number by almost 80%, killed off by decades of near-continued war. Since their rank was hereditary, there were none to take their place, no matter how much the ranks were bolstered by *perioikoi* and, later, by *neodamodeis*, the "newly-enfranchised" helots granted special status and permitted to stand in the battle-line as armored heavy infantry. In 382 B.C. this rot became apparent when, in a double blunder, the Spartan general Phoebidas led an army into the Cadmea and set up a pro-Spartan puppet government there in violation of the peace of 387 B.C. When Thebes rose up in rebellion, the Spartans also launched an attack on Athens, whose position was questionable. The attack not only failed but drove Athens into open alliance with Thebes.

After casting off Spartan rule, a democracy was set up to replace the traditional oligarchy that had dominated in Thebes for some centuries. This expulsion began the series of conflicts that ultimately led to Thebes gaining hegemony of Greece, an achievement only made possible by the genius of Thebes' greatest general and leader, Epaminondas.

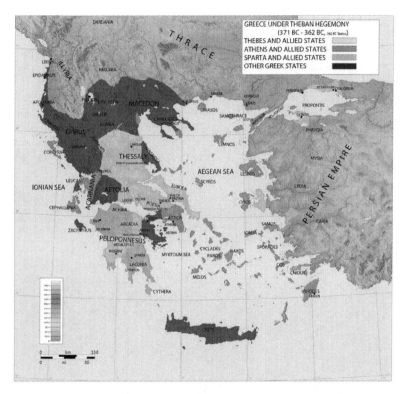

A map of the different power blocs in the early 4th century B.C.

A statue depicting Epaminondas

The influence that Epaminondas had on Thebes is hard to exaggerate. Cicero referred to him as the first man of Greece,[15] but the fact that Thebes was so totally defeated by the Macedonians only 27 years after his death ensured that he has not been viewed kindly by history. Today the verdict on this great leader is more often that his constant campaigning sapped the strength of a Greek mainland already weakened by the Peloponnesian War and thus paved the way for the relatively easy conquest of the country by the Macedonians. Pelopidas, on the other hand, has been more kindly treated by history, partly because his biography by Plutarch was preserved, and

---

[15] Cicero, *Essays*, Book II, 36.

the picture of a rich aristocrat who lost his fortune because he cared so much for the poor is an image that has stood the test of time.

Given his prominence, there are very few sources available today that can shed light on Epaminondas as a man, leader, and general. This is partly because Plutarch's biography of him has been lost. It is known that Plutarch paired Epaminondas with the Roman statesman Scipio Africanus as part of his biographical series outlining the lives of 50 figures from Greek and Roman history. That said, it must be noted Plutarch was writing over 400 years after the death of Epaminondas, and it can be argued that having this work would at best provide limited confirmatory evidence about the man. There are, however, a few references to Epaminondas in Plutarch's *Life of Pelopidas*, his great friend. He is also mentioned in Plutarch's biography of Agesilaus II, another contemporary, but the biography by Cornelius Nepo, written in the 1st century B.C., is the main source for Epaminondas. Xenophon, an avowed supporter of Sparta and Agesilaus II, did not mention Epaminondas at all, even omitting any reference to the crucial Battle of Leuctra.[16] Diodorus Siculus provided useful information and corroborated much of the other limited sources.[17]

Epaminondas was the scion of a poor aristocratic family. He was born in the late 5th century B.C., around 420 B.C. His father was Polymis, who Cornelius Nepo declared had been left impoverished due to the extravagance of his forebears. Epaminondas was a pupil of one of the last major Pythagorean scholars, Lysis of Tarentum, to whom he was devoted. According to Nepos, the young Epaminondas was a gifted student, but he also worked to increase his physical strength and his agility because "he thought that strength suited the purposes of wrestlers but that agility was conducive to excellence in war."[18]

Thus, Epaminondas began serving as a soldier, in common with other Theban aristocrats, as soon as he was considered to have left adolescence behind and become an adult. Plutarch recounted his first involvement in military action as being in support of the Spartans, though he did not mention the name of the battle. In all probability, however, it would have been the Spartan attack on Mantinea in 385 B.C.[19]

An incident occurred at this battle that was to have a profound impact on the rest of Epaminondas's life, and it was described by Plutarch in some detail. "Pelopidas, after receiving seven wounds in front, sank down upon a great heap of friends and enemies who lay dead together, but Epaminondas, although he thought him lifeless, stood forth to defend his body and his arms, and fought desperately, single handed against many, determined to die rather than leave Pelopidas lying there. And now he too was in a sorry plight, having been wounded in the breast within a spear and in the arm with a sword, when Agesipolis the Spartan king came to his aid

---

[16] Xenophon, *Hellenica*, 6.4.
[17] p. xxiv, *Alexander the Great and the Hellenistic Age* by P. Green (2007). Orion.
[18] Cornelius Nepos, Epaminondas, II.
[19] Plutarch, *Pelopidas*, 5-6.

from the other wing and when all hope was lost saved both men."[20] This incident cemented the friendship between the two men, and together the two, in due course, would come to dominate Theban politics for over 20 years.

Unlike the impoverished Epaminondas, Pelopidas was a member of a highly distinguished and wealthy family, but he was always renowned for living a very austere life, wearing the simplest of clothing and eating very frugally. He was said to be ashamed of spending more on himself than the meanest Theban citizen. His near-death experience in battle and his rescue due to the bravery of Epaminondas had a profound effect on how he viewed the world, and with his friend, he created Theban democracy.

As indicated above, the period following the end of the Peloponnesian War had proved particularly traumatic for Thebes and Epaminondas personally. The Spartan commander, Phoebidas, had taken advantage of civil unrest in Thebes to seize the Cadmea and force any he considered to be anti-Spartan to leave the city. Epaminondas, as a member of that faction, was initially exiled, but he was allowed to return to Thebes in 379 B.C. According to Plutarch, this was because "his philosophy made him to be looked down upon as a recluse, and his poverty as impotent."[21]

The remaining exiles, meanwhile, had taken refuge in Athens and regrouped under Pelopidas at the same time that Epaminondas prepared the young within Thebes itself to revolt against Spartan occupation.[22] Pelopidas returned secretly to Thebes in the winter of 379 B.C.[23] While Pelopidas assassinated the leaders of the pro-Spartan Theban government, Epaminondas led a force of Thebans, supported by Athenian hoplites, and surrounded the Spartans in the Cadmea. The following day, Epaminondas addressed the Assembly and declared Pelopidas to be a liberator, a view the assembled members readily accepted. The Spartan garrison was allowed to go free unharmed, as Epaminondas and Pelopidas were concerned that any prolonged siege would only result in Sparta sending reinforcements. The garrison did, in fact, meet a Spartan relief column on the way back to Sparta.[24]

Plutarch characterized the Theban success in removing the Spartans from Thebes as pivotal to the fundamental changes that were to follow. "The subsequent change in the political situation made this exploit the more glorious. For the war which broke down the pretensions of Sparta and put an end to her supremacy by land and by sea began from that night, in which people, not by surprising any fort or castle or citadel, but by coming into a private house with eleven others, loosed and broke in pieces, if the truth may be expressed in a metaphor, the fetters of the Spartan supremacy, which were thought indissoluble and not to be broken."[25]

---

[20] Plutarch, *Pelopidas*, 4.
[21] Plutarch, *Pelopidas*, 5-6.
[22] Plutarch, *Pelopidas*, 7.
[23] Plutarch, *Pelopidas*, 8-13.
[24] Plutarch, *Pelopidas*, 21.

The years of 378-371 B.C. were ones of success for Thebes under the leadership of Pelopidas, supported by Epaminondas. Boeotarch was the title given to the chief officers of Boeotia after 379 B.C. There were seven in all, democratically elected from seven electoral districts scattered across Boeotia. Thebes elected four, with the other three coming from outlying districts. Boeotarchs held office for one year, and failure to give up the office was punishable by death. Those elected acted as both military and political leaders.[26] Pelopidas was elected Boeotarch in 379 B.C. and he was re-elected in subsequent years. Epaminondas was also elected in 371 B.C.

Following the ejection of the Spartan garrison from Thebes, the Spartans sent another army under Agesilaus II to take Thebes back. Pelopidas and Epaminondas refused to be drawn into open battle and instead built a trench and stockade outside the city, preventing the Spartans from reaching Thebes itself. Frustrated, the Spartans ravaged the countryside, but being unable to breach the Theban defenses, they eventually gave up and returned south, leaving Thebes independent.[27]

With the field now clear, Thebes quickly re-established its dominion over all those poleis that Sparta had taken away from her. However, the new Boeotian Confederacy that was established was different than the one that had previously existed in that it was democratic. The success of the policy instituted by Pelopidas can be seen in the fact that from this point onwards, the terms "Theban" and "Boeotian" were used interchangeably.

Over the coming years, Sparta invaded Boeotia on three separate occasions. Initially, Epaminondas and Pelopidas maintained their successful strategy of avoiding any major battle with the invaders. However, the ongoing conflict resulted in the Theban troops gaining experience and confidence the longer the conflict went on. Plutarch specifically mentioned this point in his biography of Pelopidas, saying the struggle "had raised their spirits and roused their bodies."[28]

Thebes was now acknowledged as a power in the region, though not yet the dominant one,[29] and under Pelopidas's aggressive anti-Spartan policy, it was in a position to not only defend itself against Spartan incursions but take the fight to the enemy. Pelopidas secured the first major Theban victory over a much larger Spartan force in 375 B.C. at the Battle of Tegyra. This spectacular victory was mainly due to the courage of the Sacred Band, the elite group of 300 warriors that were to prove so decisive in the coming battles with the Spartans.

The war between Athens and Thebes, on the one hand, and Sparta, on the other, had dragged on up until 371 B.C., when both sides agreed to discuss peace terms.[30] Epaminondas had just

---

[25] Plutarch, *Pelopidas*, 21.
[26] *The Ancient Greeks: A Critical History* by J. Van Antwerp Fine (1983). Harvard University Press.
[27] Xenophon, *Hellenica*, 5.4.
[28] Plutarch, *Pelopidas*, 15.
[29] Diodorus Siculus, *Library*, Book XV.

been elected Boeotarch for 371 B.C. when he was sent as leader of the Boeotian delegation to the conference in Sparta. Peace was agreed, and Thebes signed the document, but Epaminondas, asserting Thebes' new position, insisted that he sign not only for his own city but for the whole of the Boeotian Confederation.[31] Agesilaus refused to allow this, declaring that each of the cities of Boeotia had to sign independently because, as far as Sparta was concerned, they were independent from Thebes. Epaminondas replied that if that was the case, then the cities of Laconia should also sign separately. According to Cornelius Nepo, the exasperated Agesilaus struck Thebes' name from the treaty, and the Thebans returned home to prepare for war.[32]

After the failure of the peace negotiations, the Spartans dispatched Cleombrotus with an army to invade Boeotia. He avoided the Theban ambushes set in the mountain passes and invaded without facing any opposition, seizing a fort and a number of ships. He then marched directly on Thebes itself. He made camp at Leuctra, and it was here that the Boeotian army met him. The Spartan army was made up of 10,000 hoplites, including 700 of Sparta's most elite troops, known as Spartiates. The Boeotians numbered only 6,000-7,000, but had the advantages of a superior cavalry and their own elite core, the Sacred Band, under Pelopidas, as well as a small force of light infantry, known as *hamippoi*, that supported the cavalry.[33] Epaminondas was in overall charge and refused to accept the advice of his commanders to retreat behind Thebes' walls. He rallied his troops by recalling the tale of a notorious rape of two local virgins at Leuctra. The two young women had committed suicide, and a monument to their memory had been set up. Epaminondas visited the monument, and suitable honor was paid to the girls before the battle. It is also claimed that he held up a snake in front of his troops and struck off its head, saying that by defeating the Spartan army, their dominance in Greece would be ended.[34]

This battle was important in another respect, for it was here that Epaminondas employed new tactics against the Spartans, tactics that singled him out as a military genius. The first action of the battle was very brief, involving a skirmish between Theban non-combatants and a force led by Hieron. The Thebans were forced to rejoin the main army, but Hieron was killed. Cleombrotus then positioned his troops in the traditional manner, employing the usual 12-deep phalanx of heavily armored hoplites on two wings. Cleombrotus, totally surrounded by his elite, 300-strong bodyguard of *hippeis,* positioned himself on the right wing. He placed his less-experienced troops, comprising Peloponnesian allies, on the left. The commonly held view was that phalanx formations had a tendency to veer to the right during a battle because "fear makes each man do his best to shelter his unarmed side with the shield of the man next to him on the right."[35]

---

[30] Xenophon, *Hellenica*, 6.3.
[31] P. 41, *Politics of Power* by H. Beck (2008). Cambridge University Press.
[32] Cornelius Nepo, *Epaminondas*, VI.
[33] Diodorus Siculus, *Library*, Book XV, 52.
[34] Diodorus Siculus, *Library*, Book XV, 53.
[35] Thucydides, *History of the Peloponnesian War*, 5.71.

Normally, therefore, commanders placed their best troops on the right side, as Cleombrotus did, to counter this effect.[36] However, Epaminondas, rather than duplicating the enemy, as was the custom, introduced two innovations. The first was that he made his left wing the strongest wing, using 50 ranks of men, and secondly, he made his lines narrower than those of the Spartans. The Sacred Band was positioned on the left, while the Boeotian allies were stationed in ranks of 8-12 men on the right. This meant that the two strongest wings were facing each other.[37]

With this alignment, Epaminondas instructed his right flank troops to avoid conflict. Diodorus wrote that he "ordered them to avoid battle and gradually withdraw during the enemy's attack."[38] This reversing of the positioning of elite troops was a totally new concept, and the tactic came to be known as "refusing one's flank."[39] Cleombrotus replied to Epaminondas's tactics by reorganizing his own lines. He moved his cavalry to the front and extended his line in an attempt to outflank his enemy. Such movements were inevitably complex, and for a time it left Cleombrotus's left side exposed.

The Theban and Spartan cavalries clashed, and the superior Theban horsemen soon had the Spartans in retreat. The retreating Spartan cavalry had to use the gaps left on their left flank by the reorganization of their lines, hotly pursued by the Thebans, who added to the confusion in the Spartan ranks. Epaminondas launched his attack and forced the Spartans to abandon their lines. At this point, Pelopidas and the Sacred Band attacked Cleombrotus's position, and the Spartan king was fatally wounded. The Spartan allies quickly lost heart and retreated in disarray, followed by the Spartans.[40] The Boeotians lost only 300 men, while the Peloponnesians lost over 1,000, but the most significant losses were suffered by the Spartiates, who lost 400 of their total of 700. This was a massive loss for the Spartans and one from which they never recovered. Epaminondas was determined to emphasize the Spartan losses, so when his defeated foes asked to be allowed to collect their dead, he allowed the Peloponnesians to do so first, ensuring that the scale of Spartan losses was obvious to all.[41] Pausanias attested that this battle was the most decisive ever fought by Greeks against Greeks, and today it is seen as permanently ending Spartan power. However, while it would lead to the rise of Thebes for a time, it also paved the way for the success of the Macedonians.

The Sacred Band

Crucial to the victory of the Thebans at Leuctra—and the subject of debate and controversy for centuries—was the Sacred Band led by Pelopidas at the battle. The Band was comprised of 150 pairs of male lovers, and this force was the elite core of the Theban army in the 4th century B.C.

---

[36] "The Supremacy of Thebes", *A Smaller History of Greece* by W. Smith (2006). Echo Library.
[37] Diodorus Siculus, *Library*, Book XV, 52.
[38] Diodorus Siculus, *Library*, Book XV, 55.
[39] Diodorus Siculus, *Library*, Book XV, 55.
[40] Diodorus Siculus, *Library*, Book XV, 55.
[41] Pausanias, *Descriptions of Greece*, IX 13.

It was totally destroyed by King Philip II of Macedon in the Battle of Chaeronea in 338 B.C., but for that relatively short period between Leuctra in 371 B.C. and its destruction, the Band's fame spread far and wide.

The earliest record of the group being referred to as "the Sacred Band" was by Dinarchus in his speech *Against Demosthenes* in 324 B.C.[42] However, most of the information now available about the Sacred Band comes from Plutarch,[43] who suggested that the Band had been originally founded by Gorgidas, a Boeotarch, following the expulsion of the Spartan garrison from the Cadmea.[44] A Macedonian, Polyaenus, writing in the 2nd century A.D., also agreed that the founder was Gorgidas.[45] Dio Chrysostom, Hieronymus of Rhodes, and Athenaeus of Naucratis, however, all cited Epaminondas as the one who had set the group up.[46]

The actual date when the Band was formed is now generally thought to be somewhere between 379 B.C. and 378 B.C.[47] There are a number of references prior to this from earlier years referring to an elite troop of 300 in Herodotus and Thucydides, and this may indicate precursors to the Band itself well before Gorgidas.[48] Indeed, modern historians now tend to discount Gorgidas as the founder and accept that there was an elite force of 300 in existence within the Theban army well before the formation of the Sacred Band.[49] In his work, Xenophon portrays Socrates as being heavily critical of the Theban practice of placing lovers side-by-side in battle, claiming that it was un-Athenian.[50] Plato's character Phaedrus also refers obliquely to the Sacred Band.[51]

For Plutarch, the Band, whether founded by Gorgidas or not, and despite the views of the Athenians, was a handpicked group selected by ability and regardless of class. Each pair consisted of an *erastes*, the lover and the older of the two, and a younger *eromenos*, the beloved. All the various writers indicated above referred to the love between the pairs, but there is no explanation as to why the appellation "Sacred" was used in relation to the Band. Various suggestions have been put forward, including that the relationship between the lovers was in

---

[42] "The Theban Supremacy in Fourth Century Literature" by G. S. Shrimpton (1971). *Phoenix (Classical Association of Canada)*, 25(4), 310-25.

[43] Plutarch, *Parallel Lives, Life of Pelopidas*.

[44] *The Boeotian Army: The Convergence of Warfare, Politics, Society and Culture in the Classical Age of Greece* by N. Ryan Rockwell (2008).

[45] Polyaenus, Book II.

[46] "The Theban Supremacy in Fourth Century Literature" by G. S. Shrimpton (1971). *Phoenix (Classical Association of Canada)*, 25(4), 310-25.

[47] 'Reconsiderations About Greek Homosexuality" by W. Armstrong Percy III. In: "Same Sex Desire and Love in Greco-Roman Antiquity and in the Classical Tradition of the West" by B.C. Verstraete and V. Provencal (2005). *Journal of Homosexuality* 49(3/4), 13-61.

[48] "The Legend of the Sacred Band" by D. Leitao (2002). In: *The Sleep of Reason: Erotic Experience and Sexual Ethics in Ancient Greece and Rome*, M.C. Nussbaum and J. Shivola (ed.s), 143- 163.Chicago.

[49] *Military theory and Practice in the Age of Xenophon* by J. Kinloch Anderson (1970). Berkley, London.

[50] Xenophon, *Symposium*.

[51] "Intra-Socratic Polemics: The Symposia of Plato and Xenophon" by G. Danzig (2005). *Greek, Roman and Byzantine Studies* 45, 331-57.

some way blessed and thus sacred to Eros, or that it was related to the vows the pairs made to each other at the shrine of Iolaus, one of Hercules's lovers.[52]

Initially, it would appear, the force was stationed in the Cadmea as a standing force to protect the city. The 300 were maintained at the city's expense, and in peace time, they trained in wrestling and dance, as well as all normal weapons training. They were also trained as cavalry, and this may have been due to the influence of Gorgidas, who is known to have been a cavalry officer.[53] The ages of those selected were not recorded, but in common with practices in other poleis, it is likely that they were about 21 when they were accepted into the Band and aged 30 when they left.[54]

In 375 B.C., Pelopidas took command of the Band,[55] and he was responsible for honing it even further into the shock troops that proved so effective against the Spartans. The first engagement of any note was in 378 B.C., right at the beginning of the Boeotian War, when the Thebans held up the Spartan attack on Theban territory. Subsequently, when the Spartans did break through into Boeotia, the Band was involved in defending the city itself from Spartan attack. The Thebans chose to meet the Spartans outside the city walls rather than retreat behind them, and the front ranks of the Theban force opposing the Spartan advance were made up of the men of the Sacred Band. A force of hoplites under Chabrias was at the front of the allied Athenian forces on the left.[56]

Agesilaus's initial probes with skirmishers were easily dealt with by the superior cavalry of the Thebans, and he ordered an advance using all his troops, with the intention of intimidating the Thebans into running away, a tactic that he had employed successfully against them at the Battle of Coronea in 394 B.C. Instead, a famous incident occurred, initiated by Chabrias, when the Spartans were only 600 feet away. The Spartans had assumed that if their enemies did not retreat, then they would advance from their positions to meet the oncoming Spartan troops on the lower ground. Chabrias mystified everyone by ordering his troops to stand at ease in the resting position, with each hoplite propping up his shield against his left knee instead of having it at the ready at shoulder height. The spears were pointed upwards instead of at the enemy; Gorgidas, who was commanding the Band, ordered his men to do the same.[57] Agesilaus was so taken aback by the move that he halted the advance. Nothing would induce the Thebans to evacuate their position, and Agesilaus was left with the choice of risking an all-out attack uphill, against what seemed to be supremely confident opponents, or withdraw. He decided discretion was the better part of valor and withdrew.[58] He disbanded his army in Thesipae and left Phoebidas, the

---

[52] "The Theban Sacred Band" by J.G. de Voto (1992). *The Ancient World,* 23, 3-19.
[53] "The Theban Sacred Band" by J.G. de Voto (1992). *The Ancient World,* 23, 3-19.
[54] "The Theban Sacred Band" by J.G. de Voto (1992). *The Ancient World,* 23, 3-19.
[55] Plutarch, *Parallel Lives.*
[56] *The Defence of Attica: The Dema Wall and the Boiotian War of 378-375 B.C.* by M.H. Munn (1993). University of California Press.
[57] *The Defence of Attica: The Dema Wall and the Boiotian War of 378-375 B.C.* by M.H. Munn (1993). University of California Press.

commander who had taken the Cadmea, in charge of the remaining Spartan force. Phoebidas quickly began raiding into Boeotia, and the results of these forays were so devastating that the Thebans had to respond. Gorgidas once again led the Sacred Band and other Theban troops, and he ultimately stopped the Spartans ravaging the countryside, killing Phoebidas in the process.[59]

Agesilaus launched a second campaign against Thebes in response, but he was once again forced to retreat when the whole Theban army came out to meet him, as before, outside the walls of Thebes. It was from this point onwards that Diodorus concluded the Thebans lost any fear of meeting the Spartans head on.[60] It was also around this time that command of the Sacred Band fell to Pelopidas, though what exactly happened to Gorgidas is unknown.

The first victory for the Sacred Band as a single unit was at the Battle of Tegyra in 375 B.C. near the city of Orchomenus in Boeotia, which was at that time an ally of Sparta. Pelopidas hoped to surprise and capture the city after learning that the Spartan garrison had gone to Locris. However, what he did not know was that additional troops had been sent by Sparta to reinforce Orchomenus. When he learned of this, Pelopidas decided to abandon his plans, but he ran into the Spartans returning from Locris at the shrine of Apollo of Tegyra.[61] The Spartan force was made up of two *morai*, with one *mora* comprising 600 men, outnumbering the Thebans by at least two to one. Upon seeing the odds they were facing, one Theban, according to Plutarch, despaired that they "had fallen into [their] enemies' hands." Pelopidas reportedly replied, "And why not they into ours?"[62]

Pelopidas's prediction proved the more accurate, and the Thebans completely routed the Spartans, who fled the field. Pelopidas did not follow up his victory, as he was wary of the large force still in Orchomenus, but the victorious Thebans set up a commemoration, a *tropaion*, on the battlefield. The battle is mentioned by both Diodorus and Plutarch,[63] and it is particularly significant in that, for the first time, a Spartan force had been defeated in a pitched battle. Moreover, it had been defeated by a much smaller Theban one. The impact throughout Greece was immense, dispelling the long-held Greek perception of Spartan invincibility. Plutarch summed up the enormity of the battle. "For in all great wars there had ever been against Greeks or barbarians, the Spartans were never before beaten by a smaller company than their own, nor, indeed, in a set battle, when their number was equal. Hence their courage was thought irresistible, and their high repute before the battle made a conquest already of enemies, who thought themselves no match for the men of Sparta even on equal terms. But this battle first taught the other Greeks, that not only Eurotas or the country between Babyce and Cnacion breeds men of courage and resolution, but that where the youth are ashamed of baseness and

---

[58] Diodorus Siculus, *Library*, Book XV.
[59] *Warhorse: Cavalry in Ancient Warfare* by P. Sidnell (2006). New York.
[60] Diodorus Siculus, *Library*, Book XV.
[61] *Boiotia and the Boiotian League 432-371 B.C.* by R.J. Buck (1994). Edmonton, Alberta.
[62] *Xenophon: And the Art of Command* by G. Hutchinson (2000). London.
[63] *A Historical Commentary on Diodorus Siculus Book XV* by P. J. Stylianou (1998). Clarendon Press.

ready to venture in a good cause, where they fly disgrace more than danger, there, wherever it be, are found the bravest and most formidable opponents."[64]

The Theban victory changed the political dynamics of the Greek mainland, and Athens began to fear the growth of Theban power as much as that of Sparta. However, the two old adversaries did continue to contend with each other, off and on, over the coming years, giving Thebes the chance to consolidate its hold over Boeotia. Thespiae and Tangara were forced into the Boeotian Confederacy, and Thebes' ancient rival, Plataea, was razed to the ground.[65] Throughout these various campaigns, the sacred Band, under Pelopidas, was at the fore. All of this success led the other major powers in Greece to conclude that Thebes had to be curbed and hence held the abortive peace conference that led directly to the Battle of Leuctra.

The Aftermath of Leuctra

The Thebans did not follow up their stunning victory immediately, but they did approach Athens to see if they would join in an invasion of the Spartan homeland. Urged on by Thessalian allies, the Thebans turned to consolidating even further their hold on Boeotia by compelling Orchomenus to join the League.[66] However, the following year, with their confidence at an all-time high, the Thebans did invade the Peloponnese. Thebes' strategy was essentially different from that of either Sparta or Athens in relation to the rest of the Greek world. A case can be made that Thebes did not seek to establish itself as the preeminent power, and that it was instead more concerned about securing its own safety through a series of alliances. By the late 370s, Thebes had secured its goals in that respect, and it was from this point that the city was ready to further expand its influence.[67]

The Athenians' response to Thebes' victory at Leuctra was ambivalent at best. On the one hand, Athens was quite happy to exploit Sparta's weakness for its own ends, but the polis was becoming more and more suspicious of Thebes. On the first point, the Athenians took advantage of Sparta's weakness to hold a conference at which all the cities of the Peloponnese were declared to be independent of Sparta.[68] The Mantineans decided to take advantage of the new situation and tried to unify their scattered settlements into one single fortified polis. All of this, unsurprisingly, angered Agesilaus and the Spartans, and they declared war on Mantinea. Other cities immediately came to Mantinea's aid, and Sparta found itself facing a confederation of the type that they had hoped to prevent.

The new confederation appealed to the Thebans for help, and they decided to support them

---

[64] Plutarch, *Parallel Lives*, *Pelopidas* 17.
[65] *Boiotia and the Boiotian League 432-371 B.C.* by R.J. Buck (1994). Edmonton, Alberta; Pausanias, *Descriptions of Greece*, Book IX.
[66] Diodorus Siculus, *Library*, Book XV.
[67] *Central Greece and the Politics of Power in the Fourth Century B.C.* by Beck, Hans (2008). Cambridge University Press.
[68] Xenophon, *Hellenica*, 6.4.

against the Spartans, sending Epaminondas and Pelopidas, both Boeotarchs at the time, with an army in 370 B.C. Once there, the Thebans encouraged the Arcadians to found a new city, Megalopolis, which they hoped would become a rival to Sparta in the region.[69]

The Thebans, with the Arcadians, invaded Laconia, crossing the frontier at the River Eurotas, which no enemy had ever crossed in living memory. The Spartans employed Thebes' own tactics against them, refusing to engage in a pitched battle while defending the city. The Thebans did not launch any frontal assault on Sparta, but just as the Spartans had done in Boeotia, they ravaged the surrounding area and freed Spartan helots and *perioeci*, hoping to diminish Spartan power further.[70] The Thebans drove farther south to Messenia, freeing helots as they went and using them to help rebuild the city of Messene. In so doing, they provided it with the best fortifications in Greece. All exiled Messenians were encouraged to return to the city.[71]

The loss of Messenia was a crushing blow for the Spartans as it accounted for over a third of the total land area controlled by Sparta and over half of the helot population, which was so vital to the whole Spartan way of life. Without the helots, the Spartans could not maintain a full-time army.[72] Epaminondas's campaign has been described as a classic example of "the grand strategy of indirect approach" aimed at destroying "the economic roots of Sparta's military supremacy."[73]

Having created two new cities to counter Sparta and all but ruining the Spartan economy and destroyed her prestige, Epaminondas led his victorious troops back to Thebes.[74] To achieve the scale of victory he did, he and the other Boeotarchs had retained their positions for several months after the allotted one-year time slot prescribed by Theban law. Thus, instead of the hero's welcome he expected, Epaminondas found himself on trial. Cornelius Nepos said that Epaminondas put up no defense but asked at the trial that, if he was executed, an inscription should be put up saying, "Epaminondas was punished by the Thebans with death, because he obliged them to overthrow the Lacedaemonians at Leuctra, whom, before he was general, none of the Boeotians dared look upon in the field, and because he not only, by one battle, rescued Thebes from destruction, but also secured liberty for all Greece, and brought the power of both people to such a condition, that the Thebans attacked Sparta, and the Lacedaemonians were content if they could save their lives, nor did he cease to prosecute the war until, after settling Messene, he shut up Sparta with a close siege."[75] The jury allegedly broke into laughter and dismissed all the charges, and Epaminondas was reelected as Boeotarch.[76]

---

[69] Pausanias, *Descriptions of Greece*, IX. The city grew over the next two centuries and at its height boasted a theatre that could seat 20,000. It was abandoned in the 3rd century A.D.
[70] Plutarch, *Parallel Lives*, Agesilaus 31.
[71] Diodorus Siculus, *Library*, Book XV.
[72] *Persian Fire: The First World Empire and the Battle for the West* by T. Holland (2005). London.
[73] P. 35, *Strategy* by B.H Liddell Hart (1929). London.
[74] Diodorus Siculus, *Library*, Book XV, 67.
[75] Cornelius Nepos *Epaminondas*, VIII.
[76] Cornelius Nepos *Epaminondas*, VIII.

The second Theban invasion of the Peloponnese in 369 B.C., again commanded by Epaminondas, achieved very little compared to the first, though Diodorus did claim that the Theban action to force a way through the Spartan and Athenian lines guarding the Isthmus of Corinth was as great as his previous victories.[77] It is not easy to see how he reached this conclusion since Thebes failed in its aim of taking Corinth after Dionysius of Syracuse sent troops to aid Sparta and Epaminondas, and they returned home only having succeeded in ravaging the countryside again.

On his return, Epaminondas was once again prosecuted by his enemies, and this time, he was not successful in his attempt to become Boeotarch for the year 368 B.C. This proved to be the only year between the Battle of Leuctra and his death that he was not elected, and he was soon back commanding Theban forces, this time in Thessaly.

In the meantime, Pelopidas had succeeded in driving Alexander of Pherae from his throne, after which he had carried on into Macedon and arbitrated between two rival claimants to the throne. To ensure loyalty to Thebes, he brought back with him to Thebes a number of hostages, including the king's brother. Ironically, that brother was none other than the future King Philip II of Macedon, the father of Alexander the Great. It is tempting to speculate that, if he had known what lay in store for Thebes, Pelopidas would have killed Phillip, who learned much from the Thebans that he used in later life (although he never learned to love the city itself). Pelopidas had to travel to Macedonia again as an ambassador, but on his return, he was taken prisoner by Alexander, and Epaminondas led two expeditions to free him. The first expedition did not go well, and Epaminondas had to withdraw without securing the release of the two Thebans being held. The following year, Epaminondas led another expedition and this time secured the release of the two men by negotiation rather than fighting.[78]

---

[77] Diodorus Siculus, *Library*, Book XV, 68.
[78] Diodorus Siculus, *Library*, Book XV. 71

A bust of King Philip II of Macedon

Later that same year, in 367 B.C., the Thebans invaded the Peloponnese for a third time. Epaminondas marched to Achaea and secured the allegiance of the ruling oligarchs to Thebes. This was not popular at home, or with Thebes' Arcadian allies, and the terms of the agreement were revised. The oligarchs were exiled, and a democracy was set up in its place. The Theban attempts at setting up democracies tended to be rather short-lived, as whenever the Thebans left, the Spartans simply reinstated the oligarchs who had been thrown out. Epaminondas's strategies would have served Thebes better, since returned oligarchs tended to be highly antagonistic to the Thebans, who had been instrumental in removing them from power. Xenophon wrote that after these abortive attempts to install democracies in the Peloponnese, the oligarchs "fought zealously in support of the Lacedaemonians."[79]

Desultory, unsuccessful attempts were made in 366 B.C. to reach a peace satisfactory to the various factions, with Artaxerxes used as an arbiter, but divisions were too deep for any real progress to be made. The fighting resumed, and Thebes itself herself in the position of losing allies to Sparta. Even the Arcadians, who had supported them so zealously, abandoned them.[80] At the same time, however, Epaminondas was successful in breaking up the Peloponnesian League, and in 365 B.C., Corinth, Epidaurus, and Philus all made a separate peace with Thebes.[81] Perhaps more importantly, Messenia retained its independence from Sparta and remained steadfast in its support of Thebes.

Nonetheless, the list of those antagonistic to Thebes grew, and Epaminondas found himself dealing with threats on all sides. He led an inconclusive naval expedition in 364 B.C., but he was unable to inflict any telling blows.[82] That same year, Epaminondas lost his close political and personal friend when Pelopidas was killed in Thessaly. In 364 B.C., Pelopidas had gone to the aid of a number of Thessalian towns against his old adversary, Alexander of Pherae. His much smaller force met those of Alexander at Cynoscephalae, but in his determination to kill the tyrant personally, Pelopidas advanced too far and was cut off from his men. He was killed by Alexander's guards.

Despite—or possibly because of—the growing opposition to Thebes, Epaminondas invaded the Peloponnese for what was to be his final time. The specific purpose of this expedition was to intimidate Mantinea, which had been working against Theban interests in the area. Thebes mustered an alliance that included Boeotia, Thessaly, Euboea, and Tegea, while the Mantineans had persuaded Sparta, Athens, Achaea, and the remainder of Arcadia to join them. The net result was that almost all of Greece was involved on one side or the other, and the two sides met on the plain outside Mantinea.

Xenophon described the battle in his history and drew conclusions about the result. "When these things had taken place, the opposite of what all men believed would happen was brought to pass. For since well nigh all the people of Greece had come together and formed themselves in opposing lines, there was no one who did not suppose that if a battle were fought, those who prevailed would be the rulers and those who were defeated would be their subjects. But the deity so ordered it that both parties set up a trophy as though victorious and neither tried to hinder those who set them up, that both gave back the dead under a truce as though victorious, and both received back their dead under a truce as though defeated and while each party claimed to be victorious, neither was found to be better off, as regards either additional territory, or city, or sway, than before the battle took place, but there was even more confusion and disorder in Greece after the battle than before."[83]

---

[79] Xenophon, *Hellenica*, 7.1.
[80] Xenophon, *Hellenica*, 7.1.
[81] Xenophon, *Hellenica*, 7.1.
[82] Diodorus Siculus, *Library*, Book XV, 78.
[83] Xenophon, *Hellenica*, 7.5.

While the battle may have been inconclusive as far as Xenophon was concerned, there were extremely important repercussions in its wake. The battle was the largest hoplite battle in Greek history, with 30,000 infantry and 3,000 cavalry on the Theban side and 20,000 infantry and 2,000 cavalry on the other. The Thebans were winning the battle relatively comfortably, but at the height of the conflict, Epaminondas was mortally wounded in a hand-to-hand fight against a Spartan, and the shocked Thebans did not pursue their fleeing enemies and totally rout them, as no doubt they would have if Epaminondas had lived even an hour longer.[84]

Cornelius Nepos argued that the Spartans had deliberately targeted Epaminondas as their best hope of winning the battle through demoralizing the Theban troops. No one is sure which Spartan struck the fatal blow, but Gryllus, Xenophon's son, is one of the possibilities. According to legend, once he knew the enemy had fled the battlefield, Epaminondas said, "It is time to die." One of his friends, in tears, replied, "You die childless Epaminondas." To that, the general replied, "No, by Zeus on the contrary I leave behind two daughters, Leuctra and Mantinea, my victories."[85] As was usual in these circumstances, Epaminondas was buried on the battlefield.

Even at the height of its power, Thebes, unlike many of the other Greek city-states (with the notable exception of Sparta), was never interested in founding colonies. This may be because Thebes was never a major naval power and was relatively well-endowed with raw materials and food. Unlike Athens, for example, Thebes never had to secure supplies for survival, so its overseas adventures were limited and specific.

That said, Thebes did become involved in areas outside mainland Greece if such involvement aided their own interests or undermined the interests of their rivals. The main external focus for the Thebans was the Aegean, and here the main opposition was provided by Athens. In 365 B.C., Athens had, at least in the eyes of her allies, broken an implicit pledge to them by setting up a colony on the island of Samos. The claim was somewhat disingenuous in that Samos was not a member of the Confederacy, and, more importantly, the Persians had garrisoned troops there in violation of the King's Peace. Athens felt that it had to react to what was a clear and flagrant action on the part of the Persians that, given the strategic importance of Samos, could not be tolerated. Nonetheless, her actions were widely resented, and Thebes stoked this resentment to persuade some members of the Confederation to leave it. Epaminondas's policy was always, where possible, to weaken any alliances that were potentially antagonistic to Thebes. Byzantium and Rhodes both left the Confederation, and Epaminondas's success in bringing important states out of the Athenian share of influence was seen as a considerable coup.

Epaminondas was extremely well thought of by ancient historians, who almost universally praised his personal frugality, his generosity, and his incorruptibility. He was, in many ways, one of the last heirs of the Pythagorean tradition that extolled the virtues of asceticism and the simple

---

[84] Diodorus Siculus, *Library*, Book XV, XV.
[85] Diodorus Siculus, *Library*, Book XV.

life. He was criticized by some of his own countrymen, particularly for never marrying and therefore failing to leave an heir, but he was clearly homosexual and had a number of male lovers and was buried with one of them, Caphisodorus, who died with him at Mantinea.[86]

He was a military genius, and even the staunchly pro-Spartan Xenophon, who had pointedly omitted any mention of him in his account of the Battle of Leuctra, commented on the Mantinean campaign, "Now I for my part could not say that his campaign proved fortunate; yet of all possible deeds of forethought and daring the man seems to me to have left not one undone."[87]

While Xenophon may have had to have praise for Epaminondas dragged out of him, Diodorus was effusive in his assessment of his military genius. "For it seems to me that he surpassed his contemporaries in skill and experience in the art of war. For among the generation of Epaminondas were famous men, Pelopidas the Theban, Tmotheus and Conon, also Chabrias and Iphicrates as well as Agesilaus the Spartan who belonged to a slightly older generation. Still earlier than these, in the times of the Medes and Persians, there were Solon, Themistocles, Miltiades and Cimon, Myronides, and Pericles and certain others in Athens and in Sicily Gelon, and still others. All the same if you should compare the qualities of these with the generalship and reputation of Epaminondas you would find the qualities possessed by Epaminondas far superior."[88]

As a tactician, Epaminondas is head and shoulders above any other general in Greek history, with the exception of Alexander the Great. One historian claimed that Epaminondas developed tactics that "marked the beginning of the end of traditional Greek methods of war."[89] In fact, many of his tactics were absorbed by the young Philip II when he was a hostage in Thebes, and they were developed further by both Philip and Alexander.

It is impossible to know what impact Epaminondas might have had had he lived longer and had the time to consolidate Thebes' power. It is possible that given the time and his leadership, Thebes might have been in a position to prevent the rise of Macedonia. The fact that his death led so quickly to Thebes' regression is testimony in itself to his importance.

---

[86] Contemporary Greeks believed that Thebes was a hot bed of active homosexuality and pederasty. However, there is very little evidence that Theban attitudes to male love were significantly different from that of any other part of Greece at that time. Bisexuality was more common throughout Greece than either homosexuality or heterosexuality. However, penetrative sex between males, of any kind, was frowned upon and diminished both involved. On the other hand, the concept of an older man mentoring a younger and embarking on relatively minor sexual interactions was considered not only acceptable, but something to be encouraged. Sparta had a very similar military arrangement in terms of the pairing of men who had close relationships to that of the Sacred Band, but it is only in relation to Thebes that the assumption was made that the relationships between the lovers went further than was acceptable in Greek society. The source of these conclusions was Xenophon, who in his *Constitution of the Spartans* 2.12 made the claim that unlike other Greeks, the Thebans lived together as if married. Whether or not the Sacred Band were the exception in terms of the normal relationships between males at this time is still unproven.

[87] Xenophon, *Hellenica*, 7.5.

[88] Diodorus Siculus, Library, Book XV 88.

[89] P. 90, *Great Captains of Antiquity (Contributions in Military Studies)* by R.A. Gabriel (2000).

The Decline of Thebes

The death of Epaminondas signaled the beginning of the end of Thebes' short period of hegemony in Greece, and it began to sink back into her position as a secondary power in the region. By 346 B.C., Thebes could not even maintain its position of predominance in central Greece and had to resort to calling on King Philip II of Macedon to help defeat the Phocians. This invitation brought Philip dangerously close to Thebes, and in desperation, Thebes succumbed to the oratory of Demosthenes and joined Athens in a last-ditch attempt to halt the Macedonians' relentless move southwards.

The Thebans were utterly defeated by Philip at the Battle of Chaeronea in 338 B.C. The battle, from the Macedonian perspective, was the culmination of Philip's campaign in central Greece in preparation for war against Persia.[90] The hoplite infantry proved to be no match for the Macedonian long-speared phalanx, and the Thebans and their allies broke ranks and fled. The Sacred Band, however, refused to surrender, and all 300 fell where they stood. Their bravery was admired even by Philip, who is said to have remarked, "Perish any man who suspects that these men either did or suffered anything unseemly."[91]

Pausanias, in his *Description of Greece*, recorded that the Thebans erected a giant statue of a lion near the battlefield on top of the common tomb of the Band.[92] In 1818, the tomb and the lion were found by a British architect, George Ledwell Taylor, and later in the 19th century, the edifice was restored by British donations to the Order of Chaeronea. Later excavations revealed the skeletons of 254 men laid out in seven rows, which are generally assumed to be those of the Sacred Band.[93]

---

[90] "Battle of Chaeronea" The Great Battles of History Ars Bellica (2015). Available online at: http://www.arsbellica.it/pagine/antica/Cheronea/Cheronea_eng.html
[91] Plutarch, *Parallel Lives, Pelopidas*, 18.
[92] Pausanias, *Description of Greece*, IX.
[93] "Observations on Chaeronea" by W. Kendrick Pritchett (1958). *American Journal of Archaeology*, 62(3), 307-311.

The statue

Many at the time regarded Philip as the greatest man Europe had produced, and he was certainly politically astute enough to assess the situation in Greece and realize that the Greek poleis were very weak following decades of conflict. However, it was really the naiveté of Thebes inviting Philip to aid them in their Sacred War against Phocis that had, in a sense, brought the wolf into the fold. The failure to confront and stop Philip's acquisition of territories, such as Amphpolis and Thessaly, due to their preoccupation with their long-standing rivalries, had already assured Macedon's victory.

Philip was content with having defeated Thebes and left it in control of Boeotia. In 335 B.C., the Thebans rose in revolt against his son, Alexander, and he proved unforgiving when the revolt failed. The city was totally destroyed except, according to tradition, the house of the poet Pindar, his descendants, and the temples and their priests.[94] All of Thebes' territory was divided amongst the other member cities of Boeotia, and the surviving Thebans were sold into slavery.

Shi Annan's picture of a bust of Pindar

---

[94] Pindar lived between 522 B.C. and 443 B.C. and was a native of Thebes. He was considered to be the greatest of the nine lyric poets of ancient Greece, and his work is the best preserved. Quintillian said of him, "Of the nine lyric poets Pindar is by far the greatest, in virtue of his inspired magnificence, the beauty of his thoughts and figures, the rich exuberance of his language and matter, and his rolling flood of eloquence, characteristics which, as Horace rightly held, make him inimitable." *Commentaries on Pindar* by Eustathius of Thessalonica.

Andrew Dunn's picture of a bust of Alexander

According to Plutarch, Alexander came to regret his harsh treatment of Thebes, so much so that whenever he met a Theban, he went out of his way to try to make amends. This most ancient of Greek cities, with a history stretching back over 1,000 years, would never recover its former glory, despite the efforts of Alexander's successor, Cassander, to rebuild and repopulate it, aided by generous help from Megalopolis, Messene, and cities in Sicily and Italy.[95]

Today, Thebes is a busy market town and the centre of a flourishing agricultural economy, but its lack of more famous ancient buildings and its proximity to Athens have made it less of a tourist site. As such, its historical significance has yet to be fully appreciated.

---

[95] Xenophon, *Hellenica*, 3.5.

For a brief time, Thebes succeeded in becoming the most powerful polis in mainland Greece. It also enjoyed key successes, most notably its destruction of Spartan military invincibility. In achieving that success, Thebes had freed Messenia and irreversibly changed the political landscape of the Peloponnese. However, Thebes' period of preeminence was too short for it to fundamentally change the inherently fragmented and poisoned relations between Greece's city-states. Indeed, it can be argued that, in maintaining the almost constant warfare that Greece had suffered for so long, Thebes added to the weakening of those poleis and cleared the way for the Macedonians to walk in and take over.

The years after Leuctra were ones in which the warring factions in Greece became ever more polarized and fractious than had been the case before. Physically, little remains of Thebes, and its legacy lies more in the tales of the heroism of its army, especially the Sacred Band. Its leaders, especially Epaminondas, were highly regarded in the ancient world, and Cicero saw him "as the first man, in my judgment, of Greece."[96]

It can be argued that Thebes' achievements were negative rather than creative, but that would do an injustice to the city that did bring a freedom of sorts to all parts of Greece. The fact that the freedoms, so hard won, could not be held in the face of Macedon's military might should not diminish the achievement, but neither can the simple fact be overlooked that Thebes did not use its power wisely in defense of Hellas.

The epitaph on Epaminondas's tomb perhaps serves as the most pertinent reminder of not only what the man achieved, but also the city itself.

> "By my counsels was Sparta shorn of her glory
>
> And holy Messene received at last her children
>
> By the arms of Thebes was Megalopolis encircled with walls
>
> And all Greece won independence and freedom."[97]

Online Resources

Other books about ancient history by Charles River Editors

Other books about ancient Greece by Charles River Editors

Other books about Thebes on Amazon

---

[96] Cicero, *Essays* II, 36.
[97] P. 254, "Epaminondas and Thebes" by G.L. Cawkwell (1972). *Classical Quarterly* xxii.

Further Reading

Readers interested in knowing more about Athens and Sparta should consult the works of Plato, Thucydides, Plutarch, Xenophon, Aristotle and Aristophanes, available for free over the internet as part of the public domain.

Free Books by Charles River Editors

We have brand new titles available for free most days of the week. To see which of our titles are currently free, click on this link.

Discounted Books by Charles River Editors

We have titles at a discount price of just 99 cents everyday. To see which of our titles are currently 99 cents, click on this link.

Made in the USA
Middletown, DE
30 October 2020